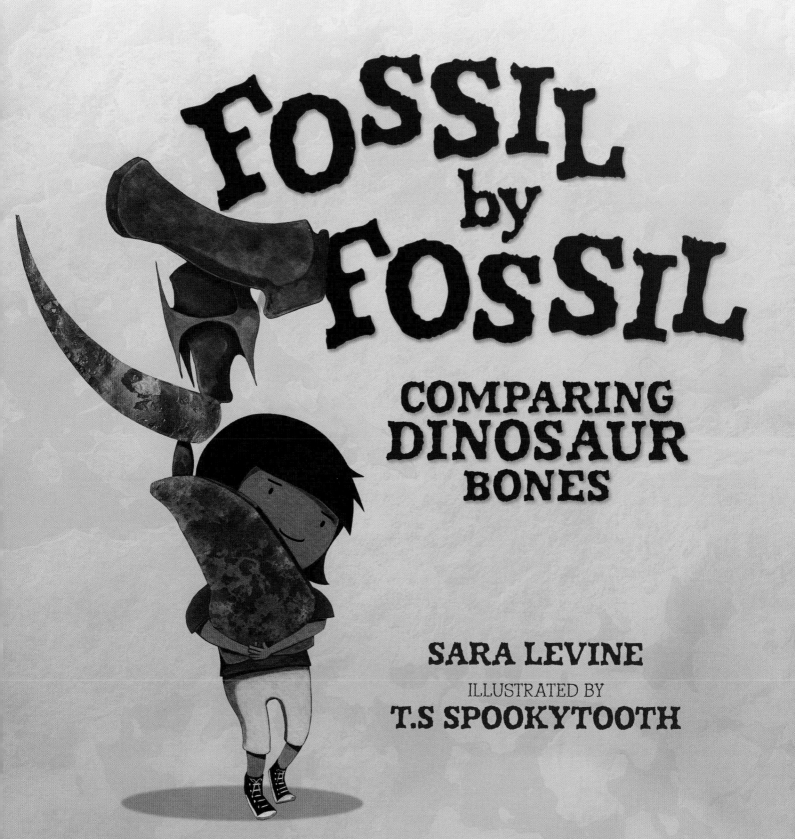

FOSSIL by FOSSIL

COMPARING DINOSAUR BONES

SARA LEVINE

ILLUSTRATED BY
T.S SPOOKYTOOTH

M Millbrook Press Minneapolis

For Benjamin
—S. L.

For Oliver
—T.S S.

Text copyright © 2018 by Sara Levine
Illustrations copyright © 2018 by T.S Spookytooth

Millbrook Press
A division of Lerner Publishing Group, Inc.
241 First Avenue North
Minneapolis, MN 55401 USA

For reading levels and more information, look up this title at www.lernerbooks.com.

Designed by Danielle Carnito.
Main body text set in GFY Palmer. Typeface provided by 29/28.
The illustrations in this book were created with acrylic paints and a little computer trickery.

Library of Congress Cataloging-in-Publication Data

Names: Levine, Sara. | Spookytooth, T. S., illustrator.
Title: Fossil by fossil : comparing dinosaur bones / Sara Levine ; illustrated by T.S Spookytooth.
Description: Minneapolis : Millbrook Press, [2017] | Audience: Age 4–10. | Audience: K to grade 3. | Includes bibliographical references and index.
Identifiers: LCCN 2017010028 (print) | LCCN 2017012747 (ebook) | ISBN 9781512498615 (eb pdf) | ISBN 9781467794893 (lb : alk. paper)
Subjects: LCSH: Dinosaurs—Juvenile literature. | Fossils—Juvenile literature.
Classification: LCC QE861.5 (ebook) | LCC QE861.5 .L49488 2017 (print) | DDC 567.9—dc23

LC record available at https://lccn.loc.gov/2017010028

Manufactured in the United States of America
1-46000-42853-5/22/2018

Can you imagine
what you'd look
like if you were
a dinosaur?

You might be pretty funny looking.
Or even quite scary.

On the outside, people and dinosaurs look very, very different.

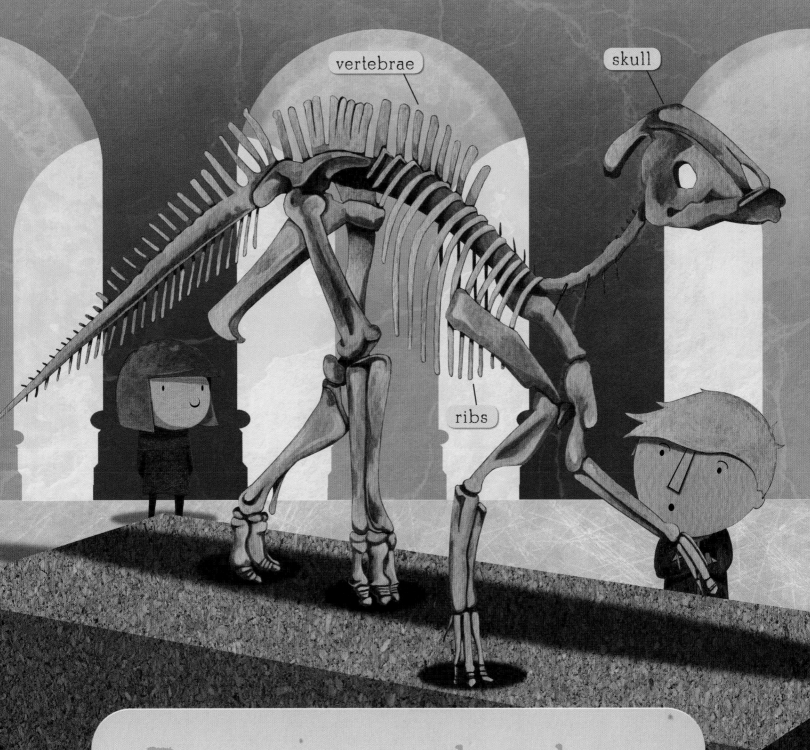

Parasaurolophus

But on the inside, we're actually very similar. In fact, the bones that make up our skeletons are mostly the same. How can we know this? Dinosaurs are all dead, right? Lucky for us, some of their bones have lasted as fossils—bones that have turned to stone over time.

Dinosaurs and people all have skulls and vertebrae and ribs . . .

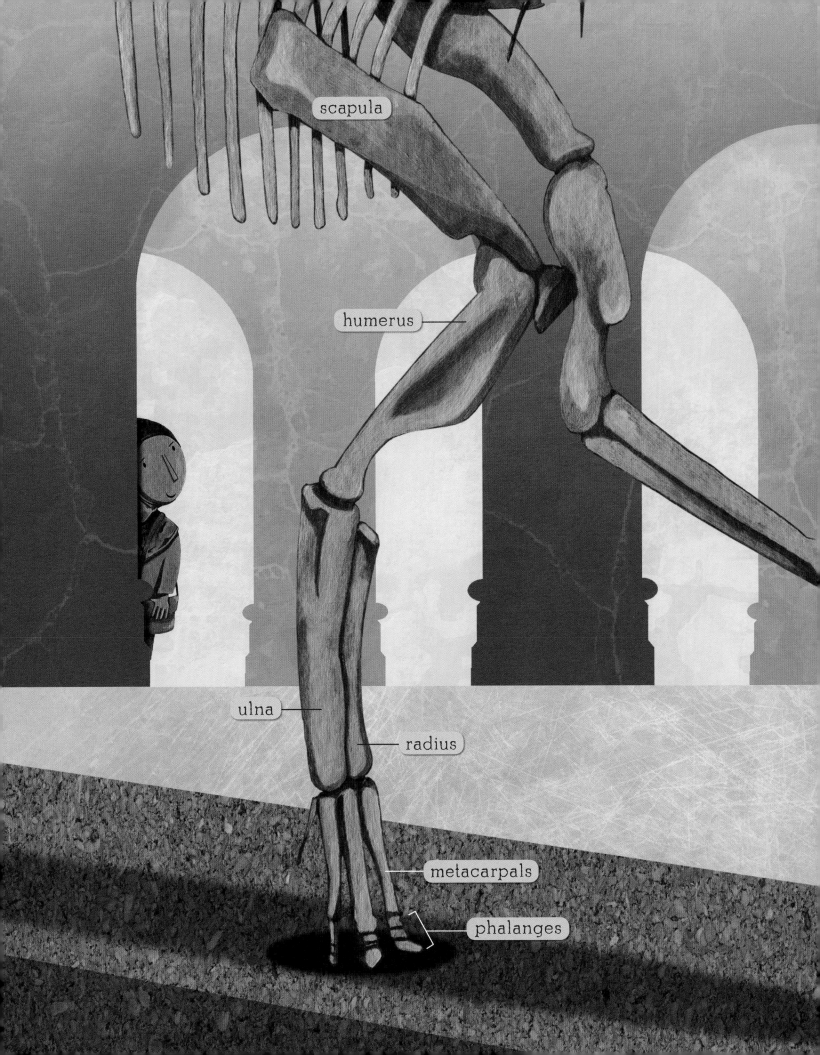

and we all have shoulder bones and arm bones and finger bones . . .

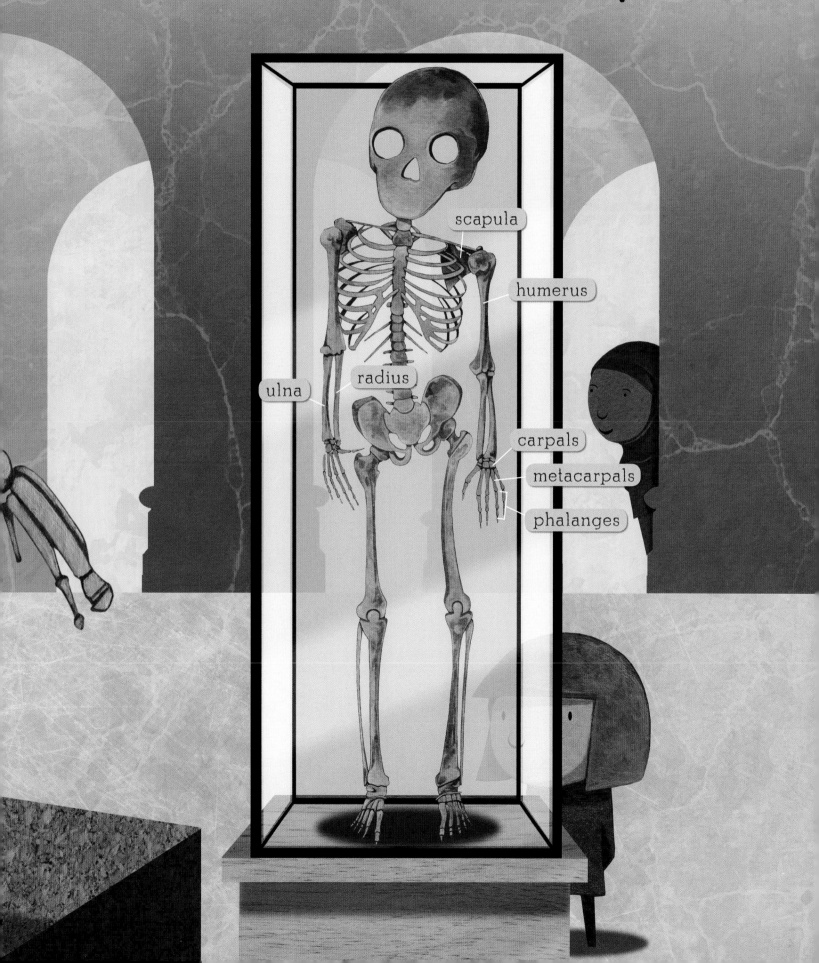

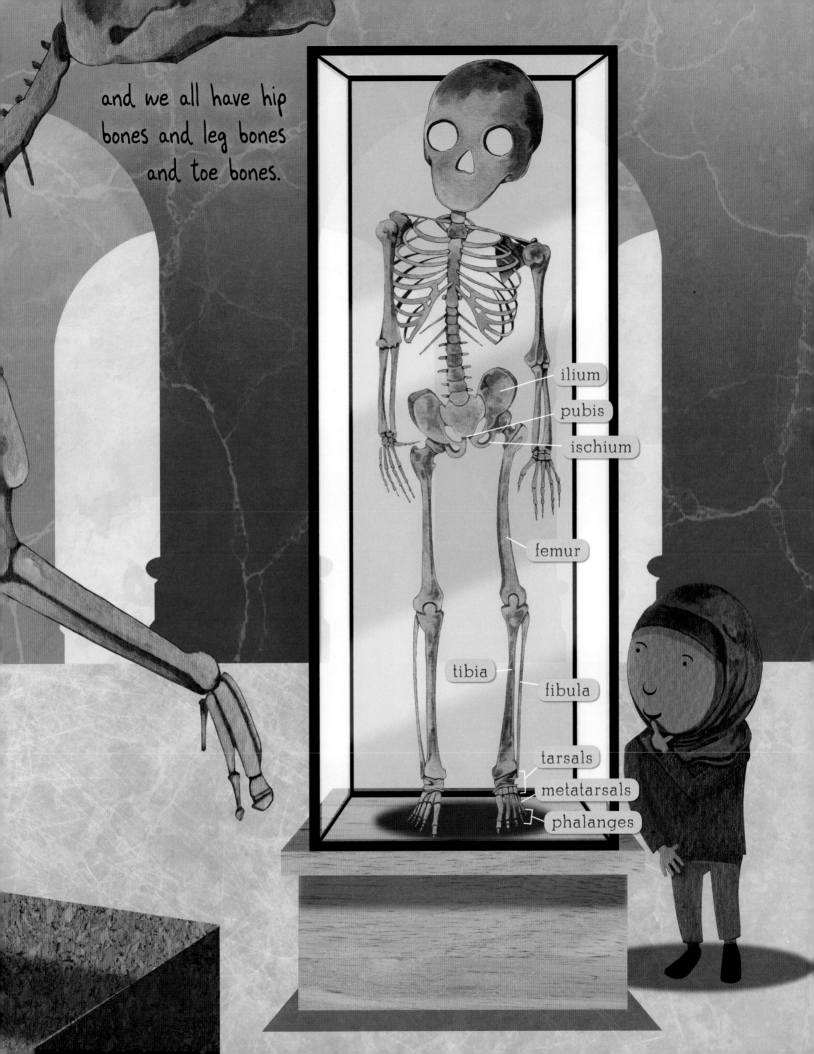

and we all have hip bones and leg bones and toe bones.

But some dinosaurs had some extra bones in
their bodies that made them different from us.

Can you imagine what you might look like
if we added some bones to your body?

What if you had a bony ridge that rose up from the back of your skull and three horns poking up from the front?

What kind of dinosaur would you look like then?

A TRICERATOPS!

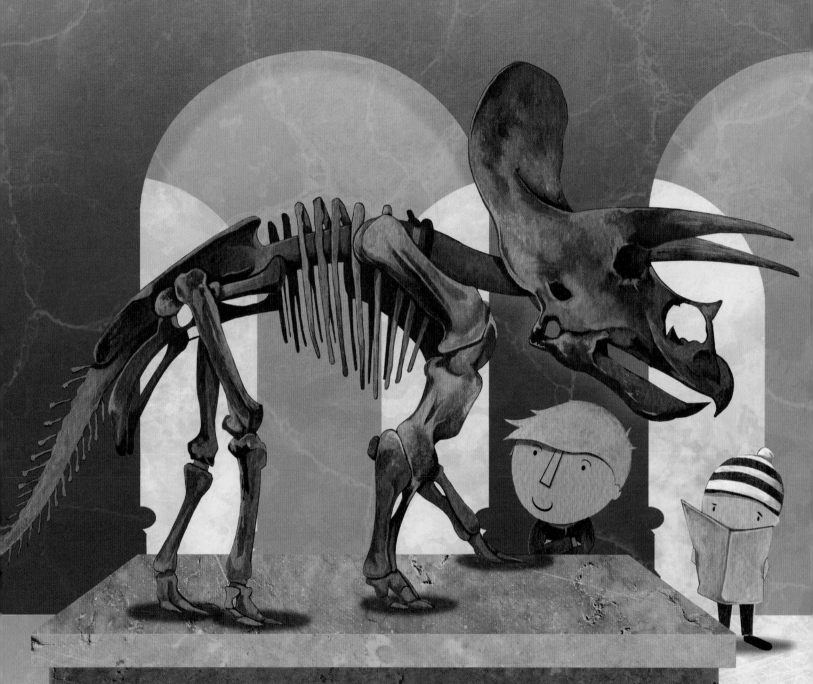

Scientists think this dinosaur used its horns for fighting.
The bony ridge in the back is called a frill. It probably
helped protect a triceratops's neck and shoulders.

What kind of dinosaur would you be if you had **rows of chunky triangle-shaped bones along your back?**

And you also had **an enormous ball of bone stuck onto the end of your vertebrae?**

AN ANKYLOSAURUS!

The bones on the end of this dinosaur's tail weighed more than 60 pounds (27 kg). That's about as heavy as the average seven-year-old kid. Scientists think that this dinosaur used its club tail as a weapon. They think it could swing—and hit—hard enough to scare off predators as big as a tyrannosaurus rex.

Ankylosaurus also had plates of bones set into its skin for protection, just like an armadillo does.

What kind of dinosaur would you be if you had flat, diamond-shaped bones above your vertebrae, starting at your neck and continuing all the way down your spine?

A STEGOSAURUS!

Why did this dinosaur have these plates of bone? Scientists have argued about this for a long time. Some think the plates helped stegosaurus soak up the sun and stay warm. Others think they might have just been there to impress other dinosaurs, kind of like a fancy outfit. What scientists do agree on is that the sharp, spiky bones at the end of stegosaurus's tail were probably used for defense.

Diplodocus was one of the long-necked dinosaurs, or sauropods. This dinosaur had fifteen vertebrae in its neck and eighty vertebrae in its tail! From head to tail, it was about 88 feet (27 m) long. That's about as long as three school buses parked bumper to bumper.

would you be then?

And you had only **two sets of finger bones on each hand** instead of five?

(Here's a BIG hint: You'd also have dagger-like teeth lining your jaw.)

What if we added lots and lots of **extra vertebrae in your neck?** And what if your **vertebrae didn't stop at your rear end** but kept going and going and going?

A DIPLODOCUS!*

* Other sauropods including brachiosaurs, argentinosaurs, and apatosaurus are also correct answers.

What kind of dinosaur would you be if your **arm bones were really small** compared to your leg bones?

A TYRANNOSAURUS REX!

This dinosaur walked upright on its two back legs like a person or a bird. Scientists think it might have used its puny front legs to help it get up after lying down for a rest. The teeth—well, you know what the teeth were for, right?

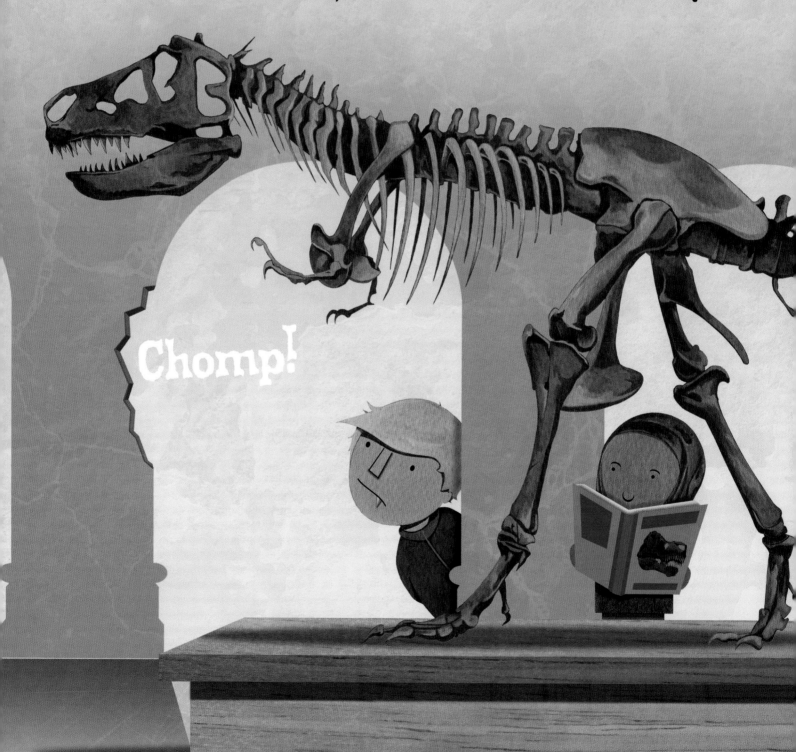

Chomp!

Dinosaurs were prehistoric reptiles that lived on land. But they weren't the only interesting reptiles alive at that time. Others swam in the oceans or flew in the sky.

Imagine that your skull ended in a **very long, pointy snout** and your **nostrils were high up on your head**. Not only that—your **arm bones and leg bones were so short they looked like paddles**.

What kind of prehistoric reptile would you be?

AN ICHTHYOSAUR!

Ichthyosaurs were similar to dolphins.

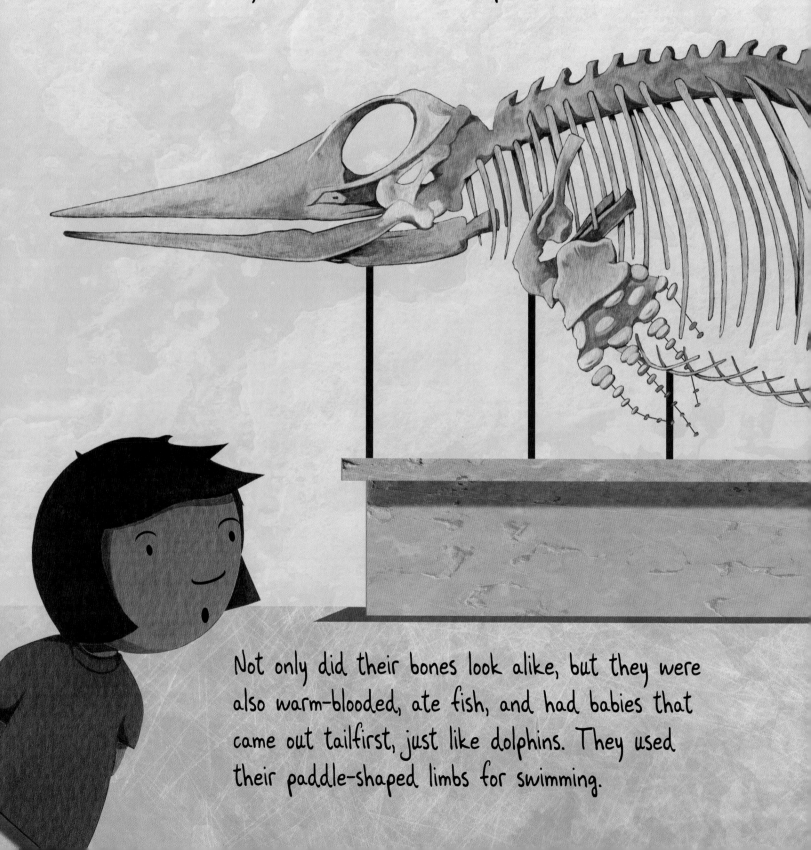

Not only did their bones look alike, but they were also warm-blooded, ate fish, and had babies that came out tailfirst, just like dolphins. They used their paddle-shaped limbs for swimming.

How about if your **pinkie bones grew really, really long** and a **membrane of skin** was attached to these bones?

What kind of prehistoric reptile would you be if this happened?

Sadly, we will never meet any of these animals in person because they are extinct. But there is one type of dinosaur that has actually survived. You may have even seen one already today.

What kind of animal would you be if you were a dinosaur **living on Earth right now?**

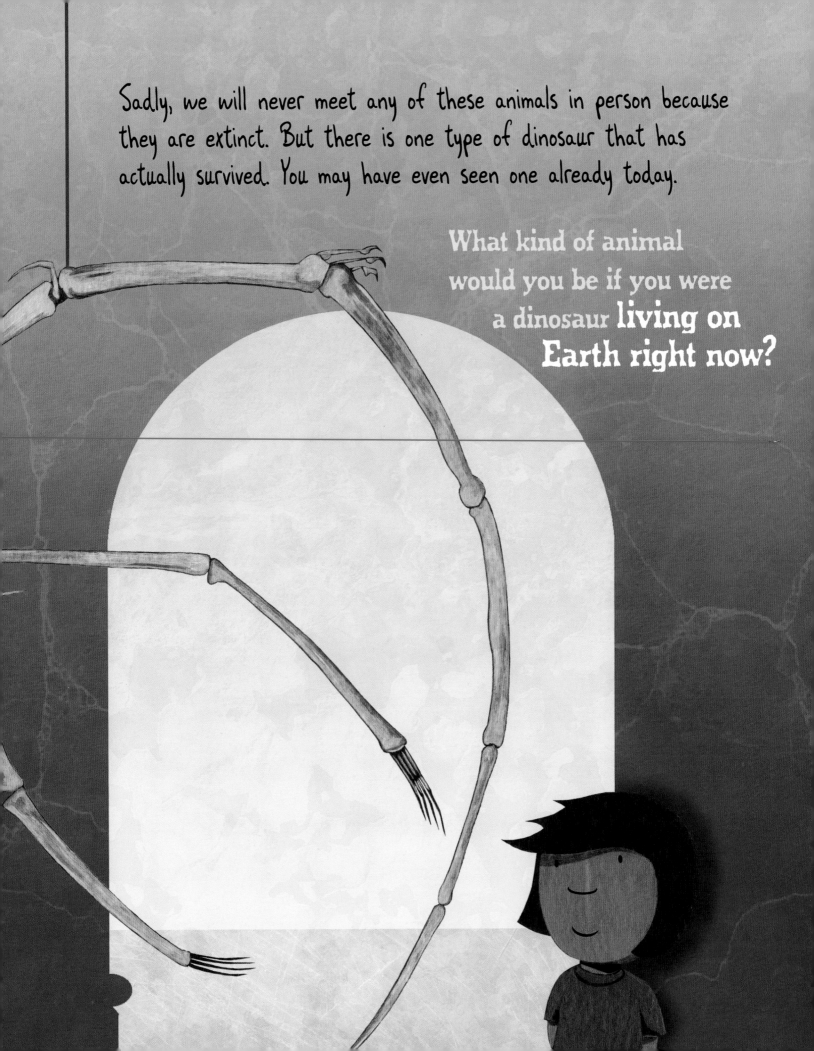

A BIRD!

Scientists now consider birds to be dinosaurs. Like the pterosaur, birds also use their finger bones for flying. But instead of flying with their pinkie bones, birds use their first three fingers.

So, if you want to find a dinosaur . . .

Go outside and look around.

You're very likely to see one!

BIRDS ARE DINOSAURS?

Yes! Birds are now considered to be a type of theropod dinosaur. Many different types of dinosaurs once belonged to the theropod group—including tyrannosaurus rex! Even though most theropod dinosaurs are extinct, scientists know about them from studying their fossils. Ancient theropods had many features in common with birds—such as having feathers, walking on two legs, having hollow bones, laying eggs in nests, and keeping eggs warm until the babies hatch. It's odd to think that you are seeing a dinosaur when you see a blue jay or a chicken, but you are.

DINOSAUR GROUPS IN THIS BOOK

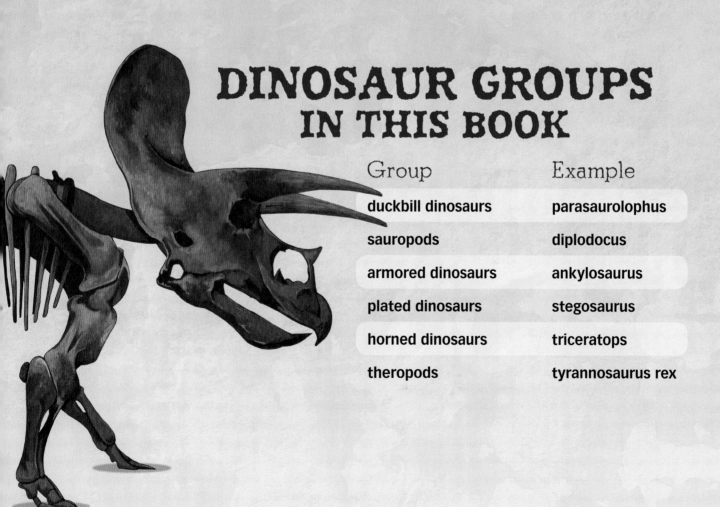

Group	Example
duckbill dinosaurs	parasaurolophus
sauropods	diplodocus
armored dinosaurs	ankylosaurus
plated dinosaurs	stegosaurus
horned dinosaurs	triceratops
theropods	tyrannosaurus rex

GLOSSARY

dinosaur: a member of a group of reptiles that lived on land beginning 225 million years ago

extinct: gone forever

fossil: the remains of an animal or a plant preserved in rock. Hard parts such as bones, teeth, and shells are most likely to become fossils. Signs left by animals, such as dinosaur tracks, are called fossils too.

predator: an animal that lives by killing and eating other animals

ribs: the long, slender, curving bones that start at the spine and wrap around to attach to the breastbone (sternum), protecting the soft organs in the chest

skull: the bones that surround and protect the brain

vertebrae: small bones, each with a hole in the middle like a bead. Together, they stack one on top of the other to form the spine.

PRONUNCIATION

ankylosaurus: an-KY-luh-SOAR-us

apatosaurus: uh-PAT-uh-SOAR-us

argentinosaurus: AR-gen-TEEN-uh-SOAR-us

brachiosaur: BRAK-ee-uh-SOAR

diplodocus: dih-PLOD-uh-kus

ichthyosaur: IK-thee-uh-SOAR

parasaurolophus: PAIR-uh-soar-ALL-uh-fuss

pterosaur: TER-uh-SOAR

sauropods: SOAR-uh-pods

stegosaurus: STEG-uh-SOAR-us

theropod: THEE-ruh-pod

triceratops: try-SER-uh-tops

tyrannosaurus rex: tie-RAN-uh-SOAR-us REX

KEEP DIGGING

Books

Bonner, Hannah. *Dining with Dinosaurs: A Tasty Guide to Mesozoic Munching*. Washington, DC: National Geographic Kids, 2016.

———. *When Fish Got Feet, When Bugs Were Big, and When Dinos Dawned: A Cartoon Prehistory of Life on Earth*. Washington, DC: National Geographic Society, 2015.

Fastovsky, David E., and David B. Weishampel. *Dinosaurs, a Concise Natural History*. Cambridge: Cambridge University Press, 2016.

Guiberson, Brenda Z. *Feathered Dinosaurs*. New York: Henry Holt, 2016.

Hartland, Jessie. *How the Dinosaur Got to the Museum*. Maplewood, NJ: Blue Apple Books, 2011.

Johnson, Jinny. *Dinosaur Skeletons and Other Prehistoric Animals*. New York: Reader's Digest Kids, 1995.

———. *Prehistoric Life Explained: A Beginner's Guide to the World of the Dinosaurs*. New York: Henry Holt, 1996.

Judge, Lita. *How Big Were Dinosaurs?* New York: Roaring Brook, 2013.

Kudlinski, Kathleen V. *Boy, Were We Wrong about Dinosaurs*. New York: Dutton Children's Books, 2005.

Richardson, Hazel. *Dinosaurs and Prehistoric Life.* London: Dorling Kindersley, 2003.

Silverman, Buffy. Lightning Bolt Books—Dinosaur Look-Alikes series. Minneapolis: Lerner Publications, 2014.

Simon, Seymour. *New Questions and Answers about Dinosaurs*. New York: Mulberry Books, 1993.

Websites

Dinosaurs for Kids
http://www.kids-dinosaurs.com
Discover facts about dinosaurs along with fun games, online activities, printables, and coloring pages.

Kids Dinos
http://www.kidsdinos.com
Information about dinosaurs sorted by type, location, and time period. This site also contains a history of paleontology and the study of fossils, as well as dinosaur games.

Museums

You can see real fossils of dinosaur bones for yourself at a museum of natural history. Here are some I visited while writing this book:

American Museum of Natural History, New York, NY, http://www.amnh.org/

Harvard Museum of Natural History, Cambridge, MA, http://hmnh.harvard.edu/

Yale Peabody Museum of Natural History, New Haven, CT, http://peabody.yale.edu